CHEETAHS

by Katie Marsico

Children's Press®

An Imprint of Scholastic Inc.
New York Toronto London Auckland Sydney
Mexico City New Delhi Hong Kong
Danbury, Connecticut

Content Consultant
Dr. Stephen S. Ditchkoff
Professor of Wildlife Sciences
Auburn University
Auburn, Alabama

Photographs © 2013: Alamy Images: 32 (Michele Burgess), 40
(Photoshot Holdings Ltd.), 19 (Tierfotoagentur/A. Winkler); Bob Italiano:
44 foreground, 45 foreground; Dreamstime: 11 (Cameron Dwyer), 1, 2
foreground, 3 foreground, 16, 46 (David Bate), 5 top, 8 (Pixworld), 27
(Sergey Uryadnikov), 2 background, 3 background, 44 background,
45 background (Snowgose); Getty Images/Christian Heinrich: 15;
Shutterstock, Inc.: 24 (Alan Jeffery), 35 (Dennis Donohue), 36 (dirkr),
7 (Johan Barnard), 5 bottom, 20 (marcokenya), 4, 5 background, 12
(Mark Beckwith); Superstock, Inc.: 39 (Exactostock), cover (Minden
Pictures), 31 (NHPA), 28 (Nomad), 23 (Prisma).

Library of Congress Cataloging-in-Publication Data
Marsico, Katie, 1980-
    Cheetahs/by Katie Marsico.
        p. cm.—(Nature's children)
    Audience: 9-12.
    Audience: Grade 4 to 6.
    Includes bibliographical references and index.
    ISBN 978-0-531-20976-9 (library binding)
    ISBN 978-0-531-24302-2 (pbk.)
1. Cheetah—Juvenile literature. I. Title.
QL737.C23M27 2013
599.75'9—dc23   2012030355

All rights reserved. Published in 2013 by Children's Press, an imprint
of Scholastic Inc.
Printed in the United States of America 141
SCHOLASTIC, CHILDREN'S PRESS, and associated logos are
trademarks and/or registered trademarks of Scholastic Inc.

1 2 3 4 5 6 7 8 9 10 R 22 21 20 19 18 17 16 15 14 13

Cheetahs

Class	Mammalia
Order	Carnivora
Family	Felidae
Genus	*Acinonyx*
Species	*Acinonyx jubatus*
World distribution	Africa, mainly in the eastern and southwestern portions of the continent, as well as those areas south of the Sahara Desert; Iran
Habitat	Primarily open grasslands, including prairies, savannas, and scrubs; some desert and mountain regions
Distinctive physical characteristics	Black stripes running between the inner corners of the eyes and mouth; coat of light tan to brownish-gold fur covered in black spots; short, blunt, semi-retractable claws; rough, hardened paw pads; streamlined body and a small, round head with whiskers
Habits	Reaches speed of 70 miles (113 kilometers) per hour when running in short bursts; communicates using purrs, chirps, growls, hisses, and bleats; no regular mating season; eats quickly to avoid having prey stolen by other large predators
Diet	Feeds on antelopes such as gazelles and impalas, as well as rabbits, porcupines, warthogs, and young ostriches and wildebeest

CHEETAHS

Contents

CHAPTER 1

Fast and Fierce

A **herd** of gazelles **grazes** as the sun beats down on the African **savanna**. Occasionally, some of these small antelopes look up from their midday meal to peer across the open plain. Everything seems quiet and calm. There is no hint of any approaching danger.

Suddenly, the still is broken by a whooshing sound. A flash of motion cuts across the tall grass. Most of the herd scatters as a cheetah sprints into their midst. The spotted **feline** hunter knocks an unlucky gazelle to the ground and uses its teeth to grab the animal's throat. Within minutes, silence returns to the savanna as this swift African cat enjoys a midday meal of its own.

The cheetah is the world's fastest land **mammal**. This cat's ability to chase **prey** at a speed of up to 70 miles (113 kilometers) per hour makes it a fierce **predator** in its African and Asian **habitats**.

Cheetahs are skillful, swift predators that often sneak up on unsuspecting prey.

Physical Features

A cheetah has a streamlined body and a small, round head with short whiskers. Its long, slender legs end in short, blunt claws. These cats typically stretch between 3.5 and 4.5 feet (1.1 and 1.4 meters) long. Their tails measure an additional 30 inches (76 centimeters). Adult cheetahs weigh between 75 and 145 pounds (34 and 66 kilograms) and are 2 to 3 feet (0.6 to 0.9 m) tall at the shoulder. Males are roughly 10 pounds (4.5 kg) heavier than females.

One of the cheetah's most famous features is its unique markings. The cat's fur ranges in color from light tan to brownish-gold. Its coat is covered in black spots that are all about the same size. Cheetahs usually have a white underside. Black stripes shaped like long teardrops run between the inner corners of their eyes and mouth. A cheetah's tail has four to six dark rings and ends in a bushy tuft of white fur.

Adult Male
6 ft. (1.8 m)

Adult Cheetah
4 ft. (1.2 m)

The tear-shaped stripes on a cheetah's face distinguish it from other feline predators.

How Habitats Fit Hunting Style

Cheetahs mainly live in eastern and southwestern Africa. Most are found in regions south of the Sahara Desert. The world's largest cheetah population exists in the African nation of Namibia. A small number of these cats also roam the country of Iran in western Asia.

Cheetahs generally prefer environments that feature open grasslands. This type of habitat best fits their style of hunting. Wetlands or areas filled with tall trees make it more difficult for cheetahs to spot prey. More importantly, having to climb branches or move across watery ground limits their ability to sprint at high speeds.

On the other hand, tall grasses and low-lying bushes and shrubs are helpful to cheetahs. They allow the cats to remain hidden from view as they stalk their next meal. Savannas, prairies, and scrubs are a few examples of places where cheetahs often live. So are certain desert and mountain regions.

Grasslands have plenty of space for cheetahs to sprint without having to avoid obstacles.

CHAPTER 2

Amazing Adaptations

A cheetah has many incredible adaptations that help it survive in the wild and chase prey at high speeds. These cats sprint in short bursts and can cover between 23 and 26 feet (7 and 8 m) in just one stride. Experts define a stride as a single cycle of motion in which each of the animal's feet is at some point in contact with the ground. A cheetah often completes as many as four strides per second. During this time, there are several moments when its entire body is completely off the ground!

A cheetah's amazingly flexible spine is one example of the physical adaptations that help it move so fast. A stiff spine would make it much harder for cheetahs to bend and straighten their legs. The flexible spine has the opposite effect, allowing the cats to take longer strides. The cat's long legs help it take these strides at faster speeds.

Every part of a cheetah's body is built to support fast, efficient movements.

A Runner's Fantastic Feet

A cheetah's feet are built to support its need for speed. Its paw pads are hardened and rough. Ridges in the skin grip the ground as the cheetah moves. This allows the cat to make quick, sharp turns without slipping and sliding. Cheetahs also have less webbing between their toes than other cats do. This allows them to spread their toes wide and grip the ground as they run, giving them precise control over their movements.

Cheetahs' short, blunt claws have a similar effect. They are also one of the reasons these speedy predators are so unique. Most cats have fully retractable claws. This means that they are able to pull their nails completely underneath a covering of skin and fur when they are not using them to climb or hunt. But a cheetah's claws are only semi-retractable. These claws continue to grip the ground as the cat sprints. Some experts compare cheetah claws to the cleats that are often found on the bottom of track shoes.

A cheetah's claws, toes, and paw pads help it grip the ground as it runs.

Shape, Size, and Speed

The shape and size of a cheetah's body parts improve its ability to sprint after prey. A cheetah's small head and slender body make running easier because they are not very heavy. They also create very little air resistance. Air resistance is the force that slows something down as it moves through the air. Larger, bulkier animals often create more air resistance. As a result, they tend not to travel quickly.

A cheetah's flat, muscular tail plays an important role in high-speed chases. Scientists often compare it to a rudder. A rudder is used to steer a ship. Cheetahs rely on their tail to balance their body weight when they run. It helps them change direction quickly without having to slow down first.

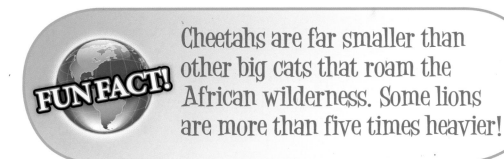

FUN FACT! Cheetahs are far smaller than other big cats that roam the African wilderness. Some lions are more than five times heavier!

A cheetah's sleek body adds to its ability to sprint at high speeds.

Oxygen and Energy

Cheetahs depend on oxygen to stay energized. A cheetah's powerful heart works hard to supply its muscles with a steady stream of oxygen-rich blood. Its large lungs, nostrils, and sinuses help it take in the extra air it needs to support this process. The cat breathes in and out twice as fast as human beings do.

Cheetahs also rely on their breathing to cool down after an intense sprint. It is not uncommon for them to pant heavily after they catch up with prey. These cats normally cannot run at top speeds for more than 122 to 244 feet (37 to 74 m) at a time. Racing farther without pausing to rest causes them to become overheated and exhausted. This is why a cheetah often gives up easily if an animal manages to escape after the cheetah's first attempt to attack.

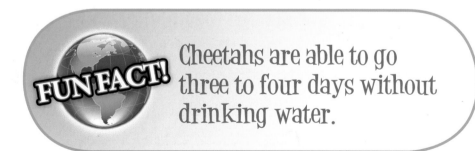

FUN FACT! Cheetahs are able to go three to four days without drinking water.

Like dogs and many other warm-blooded animals, cheetahs often pant when their body temperature starts to rise.

Exceptional Senses

Cheetahs mainly eat different species of antelopes, such as gazelles and impalas. They also sometimes hunt rabbits, porcupines, warthogs, and young ostriches and wildebeest. Their speed is only one of the reasons they make such remarkable predators. A cheetah's sharp senses are among the other amazing adaptations that help it catch and kill prey.

Cheetahs have incredible vision that allows them to detect details on objects located up to 3 miles (5 km) away. Humans find it difficult to see similar details at this distance, even when using binoculars. In addition, cheetahs have a much broader field of vision than most humans do. This means that they see more of a certain area at any given moment than a person would be able to. Cheetahs also have a strong sense of smell. However, they do not usually use it for hunting. Instead, they can sniff around to see if other cheetahs are nearby. Finally, cheetahs have extremely good hearing. They seem to be sensitive to many noises that human beings cannot hear.

A cheetah's extraordinary eyesight is one adaptation that helps it hunt its prey.

Stalking and Striking

Camouflage allows cheetahs to stalk their prey during the daytime. Their coloring blends in with tall grasses and low-lying bushes as they sneak up on their next meal. They typically sprint and strike once they are within 50 feet (15 m) of the creature they plan to attack.

A cheetah knocks its victim to the ground by using its front paws and dewclaws to lash out at the animal's hind legs. The cat then uses its canines, or pointed teeth, to grip prey by the throat until it stops breathing. A cheetah's incisors, or narrow-edged front teeth, allow it to pull the skin and fur off its victim. Its carnassials, or back teeth, help it slice away chunks of flesh. The cheetah then gulps these chunks down whole.

Cheetahs need to eat quickly. Adult cheetahs have few natural predators. However, lions, leopards, and hyenas often attack cheetahs to steal their prey.

Cheetahs are not always visible to their victims when camouflaged against tall grass.

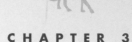

CHAPTER 3

A Look at a Cheetah's Life

Cheetahs are both social and solitary animals. They spend parts of their life cycle in groups. At other times, they prefer to live alone.

One common reason that cheetahs come together is to mate. These cats do not have a regular breeding season. They simply mate whenever they are ready. A cheetah's pregnancy lasts for around 90 to 95 days. Cheetah mothers build dens shortly before their babies are born. They usually prepare to give birth in quiet areas that are hidden by rocks, tall grasses, or low-lying bushes.

A litter is generally made up of two to four cubs. Each cub weighs between 8.8 and 15 ounces (250 and 425 grams). Cheetahs are born with their spots. They also have what looks like a silver mane on their neck. They eventually shed this grayish hair as they get older. At first, the cubs' eyes are completely closed. The newborn cheetahs are totally dependent on their mother. They drink her milk for several months.

During the early part of their lives, cheetah cubs are totally dependent on their mother for survival.

The First Few Months

A cheetah cub's eyes open about four to ten days after it is born. Within a few weeks, its teeth start to pierce through its gums. It is not uncommon for a mother cheetah to move her cubs between dens. This makes it harder for predators to find them. Lions, leopards, and hyenas all pose a threat to babies, especially when their mother has to leave them to hunt.

Cheetah cubs begin to join their mother outside the den when they are six to eight weeks old. The mother starts to teach them how to chase and kill prey. The cubs stop nursing and start to feed on meat when they are three to four months old.

Young cheetahs are very playful. Cubs wrestle and trip one another. They also stalk and strike at small birds. This behavior may seem like just fun and games. But it is actually helping them build strength, coordination, and hunting skills.

Cubs develop important survival skills as they playfully pounce on and wrestle each other.

Communication and Coalitions

Cheetah cubs stay with their mother until they are between 18 and 22 months old. They become better hunters during this time. They also learn to communicate with one another using a variety of noises, including purrs, chirps, growls, and hisses. These sounds all have different meanings. Some help cheetahs locate their mother or littermates. Others warn of nearby danger or express feelings such as happiness or fear.

Young cheetahs remain with their littermates for several months after leaving their mother. Meanwhile, they continue to improve their hunting skills and grow more independent. Females separate from their littermates when they are between 20 and 30 months old. They then lead mostly solitary lives, except for when they mate and raise cubs of their own. Male littermates frequently form lifelong groups called coalitions. The members of a cheetah coalition work together to protect common territory, hunt, and seek out mates.

Male cheetahs sometimes remain with their brothers forever.

Adulthood and the Home Range

Most cheetahs begin mating between the ages of two and four. They generally live to be seven to 10 years old in the wild. A cheetah spends most of its life cycle within a home range that covers roughly 500 to 930 square miles (1,300 to 2,400 square kilometers). This area stretches to the boundaries of where the cat regularly travels to seek out mates and hunt prey. The exact size of a cheetah's home range depends on how easy it is for the cat to find food within the location. It is also affected by how far a cheetah has to roam to follow migrating prey.

Male cheetahs are sometimes territorial. This means that they will fight other cheetahs to defend their home range. Males are more likely to behave in a territorial manner if food is scarce or if they are competing for a mate.

It is not uncommon for cheetahs to become aggressive to defend their territory.

CHAPTER 4

The Story of a Species

Modern cheetahs go by the formal scientific name *Acinonyx jubatus.* Scientists believe that they first appeared in Africa between 7.5 million and 2.6 million years ago. The word *Acinonyx* means "no-move-claw" in Greek and describes the cat's semi-retractable claws.

Fossils have revealed that a separate species known as giant cheetahs existed in Asia and Europe at the same time. These prehistoric creatures earned their name because they weighed up to 200 pounds (91 kg). A third species, the medium-size cheetahs, appeared in China between 3.8 million and 1.9 million years ago. They were not as big as their giant relatives but were still larger than modern cheetahs.

About 10,000 years ago, climate changes killed off many types of mammals. The only surviving cheetahs were members of the smallest species. These cats were the ancestors of all modern cheetahs.

In ancient Africa, people sometimes featured images of cheetahs in their rock carvings.

A Cat Cousin

A cheetah's closest living relative is the puma. These cats are also known as cougars, mountain lions, and catamounts. They are found in North America, Central America, and South America.

Like cheetahs, pumas are impressive feline predators. Both animals belong to the same subfamily of cats and probably shared a common ancestor 1.5 million to 1 million years ago. Cheetahs and pumas have certain similar physical features, such as small whiskered faces and long bodies. Yet pumas are generally larger and have solid-colored fur that lacks any spots. Unlike cheetahs' claws, their nails are fully retractable.

Pumas also have different hunting habits than cheetahs. Their powerful hind legs make them better at jumping and climbing trees than sprinting across open grasslands. In addition, pumas mainly attack prey at night and will often feed on a single kill for days at a time.

Pumas live in a wide range of habitats, including some that feature colder climates.

Split into Subspecies

There is only one species of cheetah. However, scientists have organized this species into five subspecies. The subspecies are mainly organized by geographic location.

Members of the first subspecies are found in northwestern Africa. The second subspecies lives in eastern Africa. The third exists in northeastern Africa, and the fourth roams Namibia and other parts of southern Africa. The cheetahs of Iran make up the fifth subspecies recognized by scientists.

The largest population of wild cheetahs is found in Namibia and includes about 3,000 animals. Meanwhile, Iran is home to the smallest cheetah population. Scientists believe that probably only 60 to 100 of these cats exist in the Iranian wilderness. It is difficult to know the exact world population of cheetahs. Conservationists suspect that just 7,500 to 12,000 remain in the wild.

Some cheetahs live in or near the Kalahari Desert in Namibia.

CHAPTER 5

Struggling for Survival

There is little doubt that cheetahs are fierce predators. Yet they also face many threats. During the 1800s, more than 100,000 cheetahs lived in Africa and Asia. Today, that number has been severely reduced, perhaps by as much as 93 percent!

The complicated relationship that cheetahs share with human beings is part of the reason they are likely to become endangered. People kill the cats for sport and to obtain their uniquely spotted fur. Some ranchers shoot cheetahs because they view them as a threat to livestock.

People decrease cheetahs' food supply by overhunting the same species that the cats prey on. Clearing grasslands and other natural areas to make way for farms and buildings has a negative effect as well. Cheetahs are running out of space to live as they lose more and more of their natural habitat to human development.

Hunters often keep cheetah skins as trophies or sell them to people who use them to make products.

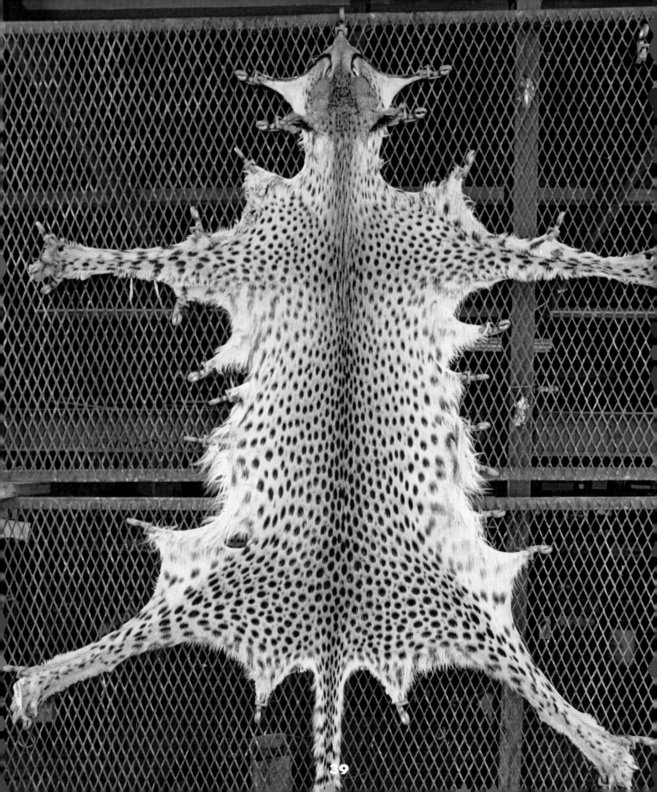

39

Efforts to Aid Cheetahs

Cheetahs also suffer from problems that probably trace back to events 10,000 years ago. Only a small number of these cats survived the climate changes that occurred at that time. Those that did survive ended up especially vulnerable to deadly illnesses and had low birth rates. Unfortunately, these consequences were passed on to later generations of cheetahs.

Fortunately, more people are starting to understand that they must help cheetahs. Perhaps humans cannot control all of the risks that this species faces. However, many conservationists are trying to educate the public about the impact of activities such as hunting and habitat destruction. Some scientists have also worked with local governments to open cheetah reserves throughout Africa and western Asia.

Hopefully, conservation efforts and greater public awareness will prove successful before it is too late. People need to do everything in their power to ensure that these unique and amazing animals continue racing across Earth's grasslands for years to come.

These scientists are carefully taking a blood sample from a wild cheetah to study later in a lab.

Words to Know

adaptations (ad-ap-TAY-shuhnz) — changes that living things go through so they can fit in better with their environments

ancestors (AN-ses-turz) — ancient animal species that are related to modern species

camouflage (KAM-o-flaj) — coloring or body shape that allows an animal to blend in with its surroundings

conservationists (kon-sur-VAY-shun-ists) — people who work to protect an environment and the living things in it

dens (DENZ) — the homes of wild animals

dewclaws (DU-klawz) — extra toes that grow on the inner legs of many mammals and that do not touch the ground

endangered (en-DAYN-jurd) — at risk of becoming extinct, usually because of human activity

environments (en-VYE-ruhn-mints) — surroundings in which an animal lives or spends time

feline (FEE-line) — of or having to do with cats

fossils (FOSS-uhlz) — the hardened remains of prehistoric plants and animals

grazes (GRAY-ziz) — feeds on grasses or other plants

habitats (HAB-uh-tats) — the places where an animal or a plant is usually found

herd (HURD) — a group of animals that stays together or moves together

litter (LIT-ur) — a number of baby animals that are born at the same time to the same mother

mammal (MAM-uhl) — a warm-blooded animal that has hair or fur and usually gives birth to live young

mane (MAYN) — the long, thick hair on the heads and necks of lions, horses, and some other animals

mate (MAYT) — to join together to produce babies

migrating (MY-grayt-ing) — moving from one area to another

pant (PANT) — to breathe in quick, short breaths in a manner that helps some animals get rid of extra body heat

predator (PREH-duh-tur) — an animal that lives by hunting other animals for food

prey (PRAY) — an animal that's hunted by another animal for food

reserves (ri-ZURVZ) — protected places where hunting is not allowed and where animals can live and breed safely

savanna (suh-VAN-uh) — a flat, grassy plain with few or no trees

scrubs (SKRUHBZ) — habitats that feature low-lying bushes and underdeveloped trees

solitary (SOL-ih-tehr-ee) — preferring to live alone

species (SPEE-sheez) — one of the groups into which animals and plants of the same genus are divided

streamlined (STREEM-lynd) — having a body form that offers little resistance to the flow of air

subfamily (SUHB-fah-muh-lee) — an offshoot of the main ranking that scientists use to classify genera, or groups of animals featuring one or more species

subspecies (SUHB-spee-sheez) — groups of animals that are part of the same species, but share important differences

territory (TER-i-tor-ee) — area of land claimed by an animal

Habitat Map

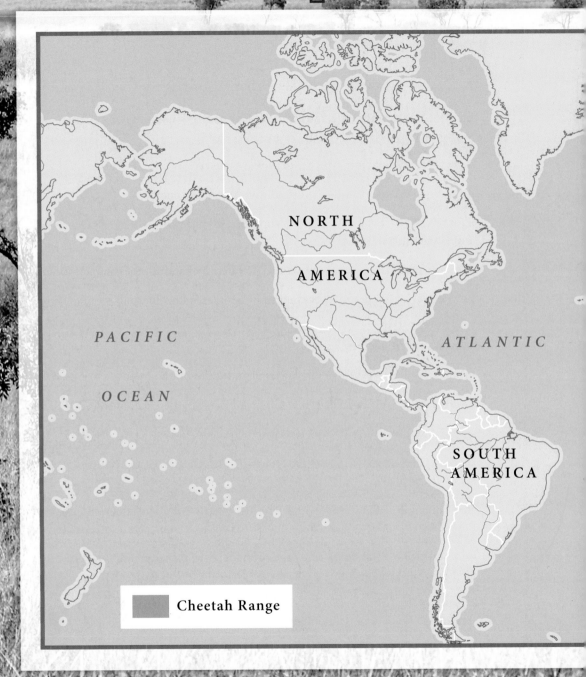

NORTH
AMERICA

SOUTH
AMERICA

PACIFIC

OCEAN

ATLANTIC

Cheetah Range

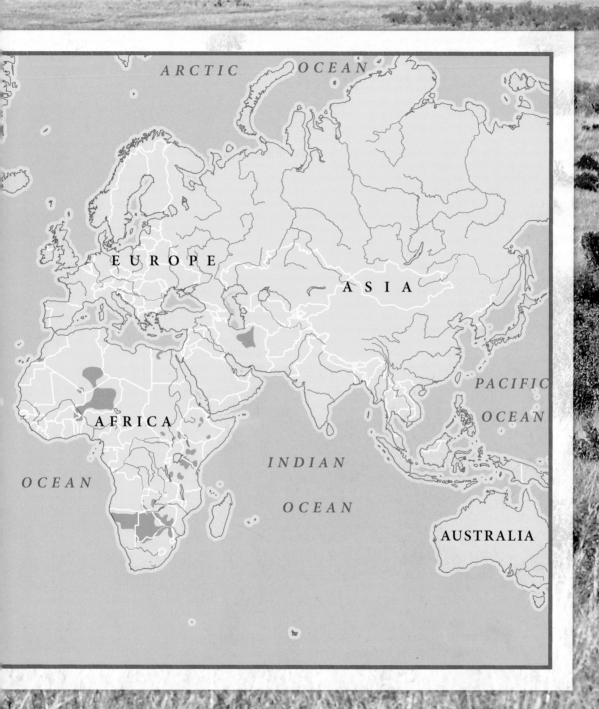

ARCTIC OCEAN

EUROPE

ASIA

AFRICA

PACIFIC OCEAN

OCEAN

INDIAN

OCEAN

AUSTRALIA

Find Out More

Books

Harasymiw, R. P. *Cheetahs*. New York: Gareth Stevens Publishers, 2012.

Reade, Clara. *Cheetahs*. New York: PowerKids Press, 2013.

Squire, Ann O. *Cheetahs*. New York: Scholastic, 2005.

Visit this Scholastic Web site for more information on cheetahs:
www.factsfornow.scholastic.com
Enter the keyword **Cheetahs**

Index

Page numbers in *italics* indicate a photograph or map.

About the Author

Katie Marsico is the author of more than 100 children's books. She wishes she could move half as fast as a cheetah when chasing after her children. Ms. Marsico dedicates this book to Christy Walker and her amazing 2011–2012 class.